The leaf boats

Story by Annette Smith
Illustrations by Naomi C. Lewis

2

Matthew and Emma
ran down to the water.

They looked at the big boys
and they looked at the boats.

4

"Here comes the big red boat," shouted Emma.

"It will win the race."

"No!" said Matthew.

"Look at the yellow boat. It is winning!"

"Oh, look!" said Matthew.
"The big boys are going away
with the boats."

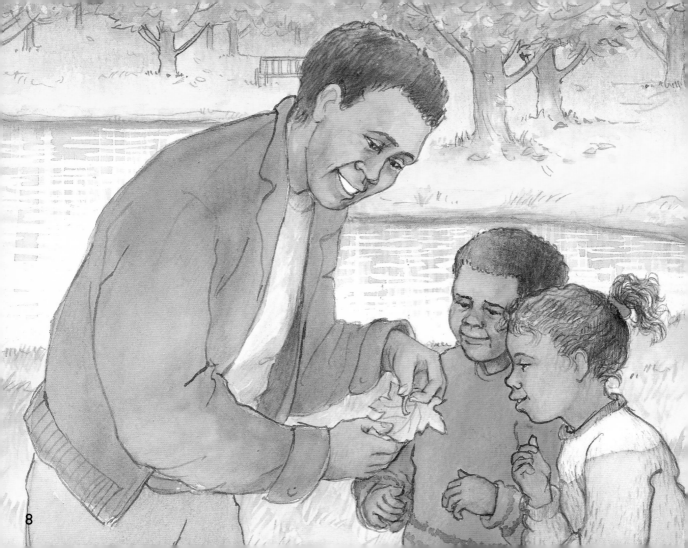

8

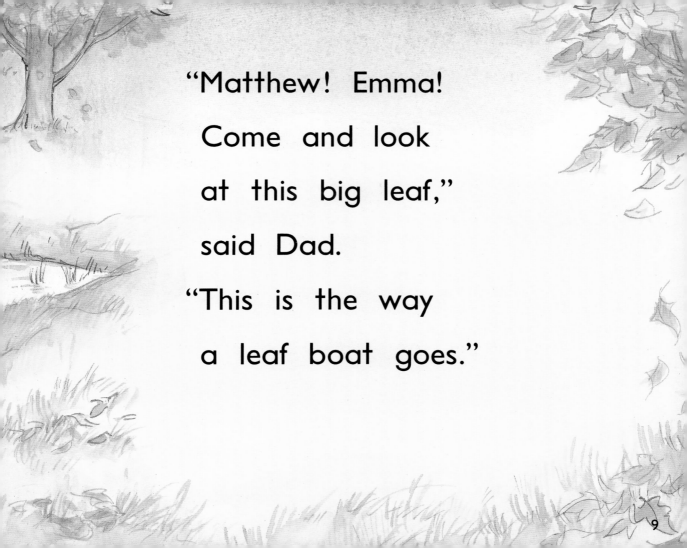

"Matthew! Emma!
Come and look
at this big leaf,"
said Dad.
"This is the way
a leaf boat goes."

9

"Matthew, here is a boat
for you," said Dad.
"And here is your boat, Emma."

Matthew said,

"Here is **your** leaf boat, Dad."

"The boats can go in a race,"
said Emma.

"My boat will win!"
shouted Emma.

"No! Look at my boat!"
said Matthew.

"Oh! Look at Dad's boat!"

"Here come the winners,"
shouted Dad.

16